GROWING
THE REAL ME

GROWING
THE REAL ME

The Raw and Undeniable Story of a
Schizophrenic Coming Into Reality

SHIRANA JOY
with Christine E.

O'LEARY
PUBLISHING
The Influencer's Press

NAPLES, FL

Published in the United States by
O'Leary Publishing
www.olearypublishing.com

The views, information, or opinions expressed in this book are solely those of the authors involved and do not necessarily represent those of O'Leary Publishing, LLC.

The author has made every effort possible to ensure the accuracy of the information presented in this book. However, the information herein is sold without warranty, either expressed or implied. Neither the author, publisher, nor any dealer or distributor of this book will be held liable for any damages caused either directly or indirectly by the instructions or information contained in this book. You are encouraged to seek professional advice before taking any action mentioned herein.

For information on wholesale orders or getting permission for reprints and excerpts, contact: O'Leary Publishing at admin@ olearypublishing.com

ISBN: (print) 978-1-952491-88-7
ISBN: (ebook) 978-1-952491-89-4

Cataloging–in–Publication Data is on file with the Library of Congress.

Developmental Editing by Heather Davis Desrocher
Line Editing by Jennifer Doody
Proofreading by Kat Langenheim and David Aretha
Cover and Interior Design by Jessica Angerstein

Printed in the United States of America

This book is dedicated to all
suffering schizophrenics.

Contents

Part III – Growing Into Reality

JANET

a Poem
by Steve

There once was a woman named Janet[1]

who had trouble staying on the planet.

She traveled dimensions

but without conventions

thinking the 4th (dimension) her invention.

The 3rd was the goal

for this wandering soul.

The 4th would steal good intentions.

Now if there weren't enough

for this wench of "right stuff,"

let me tell you about the black hole.

Out of time,

out of space,

Would she quickly race

when the black again got to her soul

---

1 Janet was the name that Shirana was born with.

when the tear sneaks up,

her brain goes to gup.

Though to stay is the point,

she just leaves the joint

without knowing that to stay

is okay.

"Stop her," you say, and I think you are right.

But nothing I've done has prevented her flight.

I know in myself that soon, soon she'll be back.

Her heart in her hands, her soul and her act.

Give us this day our daily bread

and save Dear Janet, this awful dread.

February 4, 1989

The First Meeting
by Christine E.

As I waited for my new client to arrive, I considered what the colleague who had sent her to me had said, "Janet is a PK (preacher's kid) with some religious trauma." I was known as both a Christian therapist as well as a trauma specialist, and my colleague thought I would be a good fit for Janet. My schedule was very full, but I agreed to see her for a short time.

When Janet arrived, I immediately knew that her issues went far beyond religious trauma, although I didn't know the nature or scope of what she was presenting. Janet (Shirana) was in her forties – five years older than I was – but possessed a strange, childlike quality. She was dressed in her letter carrier uniform, and I was immediately drawn to her state of neglected personal hygiene. I had to adjust my focus away from the unwashed smell and newsprint-stained hands to the soul standing in front of me – the beautiful and tortured soul.

Her eyes, when they met mine, were tentative but determined. I could see the intelligence and the depth of her mind, as well as the courage it took to start something new. Immediately she asked me if she could go around the room and touch various objects to *make them real* and I agreed. She took her time perusing the items on my bookshelves and tables, holding each item in her hands and looking at it intently.

After she finished, she sat down and we began. She picked up the Christmas bear that was sitting on the back of the couch and clutched it tightly as we talked. She made eye contact occasionally, but she frequently looked off to the side or down at her feet.

I asked her a variety of questions, which she answered, but many of her answers were, "I don't know or I don't remember." I was able to get some family history, but she frequently said, "That wasn't real to me."

She also fidgeted a lot with her hands, clenching and unclenching as we talked. We finished the session and set up another time. Little did I know that "a short time" would turn into over thirty years of working together and becoming like family.

EDITORIAL NOTE
TO THE READER

This story is written in Shirana's voice with as little editorial adjustments as possible. We want you to experience her as authentically as we have during the process of collaborating with her to bring forth this book. She is a truly delightful human being with much to offer. We hope you enjoy her story and feel a profound sense of hope no matter how schizophrenia has touched your life, personally or professionally.

PART 1

Mimicking Everyone

Reflection on Schizophrenia

Imagine a world where nothing is real – where you have to touch things and pick them up just to learn that they are real. Imagine not experiencing emotion, connection, love, or understanding. Imagine how isolating that would feel, every hour of every day, in every situation. That was my life. I was disconnected from reality because I was schizophrenic.

For those who have not experienced schizophrenia themselves, this may sound strange. How could I not be my real self in the real world? But most people know nothing about how a person with schizophrenia functions or survives. As a schizophrenic, I didn't feel. I had no healthy connections with anyone. I functioned from a false self, as I had learned to mimic other people. I lived my entire life from a programmed script in which

I had to intuit and adapt in every moment. It wasn't real to me. Nothing felt real. But pretending, in every moment, helped other people accept me. I became so good at pretending and looking okay – out of the need to survive – that people did not believe just how far disconnected I was.

Since my birth, I lived beneath the earth in an inky, black pit with absolutely nobody around anywhere. I was profoundly alone. When I looked up from that pit, I could see people on solid ground bathed in white light, walking, holding hands, laughing, the sun pouring down on them (like the image on the cover of this book). But that was totally the opposite of what I was experiencing.

Most people are in the real world, where they have experiences. Schizophrenics do not have real experiences because we are not in reality. It may look as if we are, but we are not. We are totally disconnected from others, and to us our real selves do not exist on the outside or on the inside.

I have been working for years to heal this disconnection, and I have learned a great deal. In my experience, the largest factor in creating schizophrenia is a lack of the initial, emotional connection with the mother – even as early as the entrance into the womb. I have learned through years of experience that traditional therapy does not work with schizophrenics, because it does not go back far enough to where they disconnected – likely in the womb.

The effort to come out of schizophrenia was a battle that demanded 100 percent from me. It took incredible willpower from every cell of my being. As an adult, I worked with many different therapists. I even did soul retrieval work with one therapist who took me back far enough to remember the beginning of this life.

After decades of therapy, I found a way to step into reality and allow my true self to emerge. It was not easy, but it was worth it for the life I am living today. Now, I am out of the pit, walking on the solid earth beneath me; I can feel sunlight pouring down on me. I am feeling, growing, laughing – I am relating to people and they are relating to me. The split within me, the false self I have presented to the world to survive, is melting away. My real, true self is coming out and filling up my insides. It is a miracle – a complete transformation and an entirely different experience.

It is almost impossible to put this shift into words. After being truly numb for my whole life, I can now have what most people take for granted: safety, emotions, authenticity, love, and peace. Living in reality is truly a miracle; and if I can do it, others can, too. And so I want to share my journey – this miracle – to help others who may be living in the strange, disconnected world of schizophrenia.

This is my true, raw, and unfiltered story.

The Womb Experience

When I read books about life after death, which I love to read, everything they say about transitioning to the heavens happened to me, only I was transitioning into the earth plane. I was up in the inky black sky, and I looked down to the earth and there were two people in the dark copulating (that's the word that went through my mind). I was horrified because it looked very cold and dark. I was shocked, and I turned back and God was there. He was bathed in white light, lying on a throne couch. The way people talk about shooting thoughts back and forth in the place of words – that's exactly what we did.

I shot the thought to him: *I can't survive down there.*

He looked at me with great, great gentleness and a half smile and shot back, *That's your next assignment.*

It was also very clear what I felt and wanted was not going to interfere with my next assignment. The universe and God had predetermined my next assignment.

And then, I was shot down and all of a sudden I was in her stomach. It was a total shock.

I knew I needed to reach up to physically connect with the woman I was inside of and attach emotionally – and I tried. But there was this incredible amount of rage pouring down on me in waves – loads of limitless rage. It was coming from her, although she was totally oblivious to the fact that I was there inside of her. What is amazing is that many mothers are totally unaware of conception when it is happening. A woman often does not even know that she has conceived. When I was shot into the womb, I was precisely aware of how oblivious she was to my existence.

Then I realized there was someone else in the womb with me – my twin. He had already figured out what was going on and had turned around and faced the inside of the womb. I tried to reach out and attach to him, but there was no way I could.

After that realization, I knew that there was no way I could physically survive without putting my real self, and my heart, away.

So the timeless part of me, I will call her the Ancient Being, reached in, took the self out of my chest, and put it under the floor so my mother could not find it. The Ancient Being knew that this was the only way I would and could survive physically – by hiding my real self away.

After I was born, I was in a crib on the floor next to the bed where Mrs. Hess was (this is what I call my birth mother because it gives me critical emotional distance from her). She was up there in the light and there were nurses around her who were talking. Mrs. Hess was totally oblivious to the fact that I was there on the floor. She had no interest in picking up the baby to love it – like mothers do in the movies. It was total disassociation and non-attachment to me. She was utterly disinterested and there was this being, whom I call Him, who knew it, and he took advantage of her disinterest.

Silently, Him showed up in the corner of the room. I saw Him right away and he saw me. I knew that he was not allowed to come into me for 20 minutes. Mrs.

Hess had 20 minutes to pick me up and bring me into the real world to belong there. I knew she never would, but we just had to silently wait there for the 20 minutes to pass.

And then Him came in and took me over exactly at 20 minutes. He was like a cover over me all of my life, until I eventually, through a ritual, was able to send Him back to the light.

The Hess Family

John, my twin, was 25 minutes older than me. I was always proud of being a twin, but it never seemed to matter to him at all. While we were growing up, he felt disconnected from me. It's like he went through the motions and he did what he needed to do, but he was the same as when we first met in the womb: cold and withdrawn. Looking back at my womb experience, I think I responded so drastically in the womb because I was far more emotionally aware than my twin of the level of rage pouring down on me in the womb. I had to disconnect from myself more in order to physically survive.

There were four children in our family. My brother Dan was six years older, and my sister Deborah was three years older. My parents and my siblings would talk among themselves – I wasn't attached to any of them. They saw me as this horrific thing that was always tormenting everyone. Things were always my fault. They talked about me behind my back and decided horrible things about me. I learned this years later when I was a lot more attached to reality and I understood more about what had been going on. But they never communicated with me directly, which I think is one of the biggest causes of schizophrenia: lack of direct relatedness and communication. I never existed to any of them in a positive way as a real person. Nobody in the family asked me how I felt or where I was. I called my parents Dr. and Mrs. Hess to keep them far away and keep me safe emotionally. No one in my family ever related to me. No one ever asked me anything about myself. I was just given this program I was supposed to follow and that was it.

My sister was more connected to Mrs. Hess, who used to be in bed all the time because she was quite *sick*. After school my sister would go and lie on Mrs. Hess' bed and talk with her. I was never attached enough to Mrs. Hess to ever do that. I think my sister received more nurturing at the beginning of life from Mrs. Hess because there were only two children. When John and

I came along, there were four children, three of whom were three years old or younger.

When I felt the rage from Mrs. Hess all through my childhood, the Ancient Being was watching out for me, being hypervigilant, keeping me alive. Everything that this ancient soul did was to keep me alive – she was a part of me, protecting the real me. It was the spirit part of me that had gone through thousands of emanations that had that profound ancient wisdom. I would just listen to everything she would say. SHE saved my life **many** times!

Mrs. Hess

Mrs. Hess (our mother) hardly did anything for us. Some books on schizophrenia say that the mothers are very cold and icy – others say it's just biological. In my experience, the mothers of schizophrenics are incredibly cold and icy.

Mrs. Hess got out of doing most things. Meals were very rigid in our house. Dr. Hess would fix the breakfast before school while Mrs. Hess was *sick* in bed. Lunch was at 12:30. Dinner was at 6:00. We were not allowed to go to the refrigerator or to get any food, even if we were hungry. So I grew up hungry. We weren't poor, but I was physically hungry, so it feels like I grew up starved.

Because my father was a minister my mother wasn't allowed to have any problems. But she had problems with her thyroid and was in bed all the time. When she had to do anything related to being a mother she was miserable. If she had to make dinner she would lean on one leg and moan miserably, and then lean on the other leg and moan again, like it required so much effort.

Usually, Auntie Helen (who was not my real aunt), a lady in the church, came and cooked dinner for us after she finished her day job. Auntie Helen was warm and wonderful. She had a wonderful laugh and showed an interest in me, which was a shock. I couldn't feel it or connect, but I could see that she was a safe and real person. In addition to making dinner for us, sometimes she would also come in the morning to help us. I don't think she was ever paid. Dr. Hess had people in the church do things for us because "they were doing it for the Lord."

When it came to reading and writing, Mrs. Hess was fine. She taught a Bible class and there were hundreds of people in it. When she was preparing for her Bible class in the study, she was calm and efficient, sitting up straight. No moans, no heavy dramatic sighs. She was like a totally different person, which I always wondered about.

Mrs. Hess never showed the slightest interest in normal mom things. I had no idea that parents would dress their children up for Halloween or go out to trick-or-treat with them. I took care of it myself. I would find a sheet and cut holes in it and make myself into a ghost. John and I would leave the house together on Halloween night, but he had no interest in relating. When we were halfway down the sidewalk he would run ahead and he was gone. So I went trick-or-treating all by myself. I collected as much candy as I could (since I stayed alive by eating candy in a house where food was rationed). I ended up rotting my teeth with all of the candy.

Mrs. Hess was rigid about things and insisted that I take piano lessons. She would sit next to me, trying to make me practice, and I would get really, really upset. All that mattered in our house was that I produced – I was never real as a person. It was also absolute that we did well in school. In 10th grade I got a D in algebra and this was **ABSOLUTELY** not okay in the Hess family. Years later I found out that my parents had gone and talked to the principal to make sure that I would not take any more hard classes like chemistry or physics.

They did not want to take a chance of me having bad grades, which made them look bad. But they **never** talked to me at the time about what they did!

During this time, when I was in high school, I was angry a lot of the time – I was an enraged teenager. I did not know it at the time, but it is common for schizophrenics to experience rage when they are teen-agers. When I read about this in a book as an adult, it was very comforting. I always felt so different from others, like something was very wrong with me. It was nice to know that the way I was had a reason.

***

When I was about four, Mrs. Hess was on her hands and knees scrubbing the kitchen floor and, according to her, all of a sudden she felt something snap – it was her health breaking. And then she had to go down to Florida for six weeks.

While Mrs. Hess was away, John and I were sent to live with the Martinecs, a couple from church. From the moment I got there, they felt real. There were many rules in their house. We could not get up until 9:00 in the morning. We had to sit on the toilet until we had gone number one and number two. My brother could do that very easily but I couldn't. So I had to sit on that toilet for a long time. Although that might seem harsh to some, all I felt was love, for the first time. They did it because they cared about me and loved me. I had **never** experienced that before!

When we had breakfast Arthur Godfrey was on the radio and I would listen to him every morning. (Most things I do not remember well, but this has been incredibly vivid to me throughout my life.) I rode a tricycle up and down the sidewalk and felt good about it. I don't remember anything like that in my household. It was the only time I ever felt love. Normal people say, "My parents made mistakes, but they loved me." Well, I didn't know what that meant, because that was not my experience. But with the Martinecs I could feel love. After six weeks Mrs. Hess came home and we went back, and everything inside of me went blank again.

As an adult I found out what really happened to Mrs. Hess when I was four. I was going to my brother's wedding with my mother's younger sister, Aunt Tizzy, who was a wonderful person. I told her the story of Mrs. Hess' health breaking and she said, "What?"

I repeated the story and Aunt Tizzy roared with the most natural, spontaneous laughter. She said, "Everyone knows that your mother had a nervous breakdown." That was the biggest gift anybody could have ever given me – the truth. Before this conversation, if something went wrong in my family it had always been all my fault. I believed that I had not been made right as a person. What Aunt Tizzy did was to put some responsibility on others – it was no longer all my fault. It was so comforting to learn this. Once again, I believe a cause of schizophrenia is an **utter** lack of real relatedness and communication as if a person does not exist in an autonomous or positive way.

Dr. Hess

Dr. Hess thought that he was more clever and better than everybody else. He skipped fourth and seventh grades and graduated from high school when he was 12. He graduated from college when he was 15 and earned a PhD by the time he was 21.

His father was a Presbyterian minister who had OCD (obsessive-compulsive disorder). He preached in small country churches and they moved often. From the stories I heard, my grandfather appeared to be a wonderful man of God, but he was not. When he was preaching he would say things like, "Now don't do this like Mrs. So-and-So does." It would be a negative thing and Mrs. So-and-So would get very upset and have him kicked out of his position as the minister.

So every two years or so, my father and his family would have to move and start over. That must have affected Dr. Hess' emotional growth, especially if he went to college when he was 12. But nobody ever talked to me about these things. When I tried to talk to my sister about it as I grew into an adult, she did not acknowledge anything.

The only memory I have of my father's father is when he gathered up all the children and walked us a few blocks to an old cement pool to go fishing. I had never experienced anyone paying attention to children like that before. It was mystifying to me. The whole family despised my grandfather as a worthless loser, but that was not what I experienced. I wonder now if the negative family view of him was because he was kind to children.

My father's mother was brutal and harsh and demanding. She was also a minister and preached sometimes. One time my grandparents came to visit us in Cicero, Illinois, and my grandmother was preaching in a church service. My twin John was sitting in the second row with some friends. I was sitting across from him on the other side of the aisle. Evidently John and his friends were disruptive and my grandmother stopped in the middle of the sermon, pointed at John, in front of everyone, and said, "John, cut it out!" And then she went on with her sermon. The harshness and the condemnation in front of others (the whole congregation) was familiar, which made it more real than anything else. I was so glad I was not sitting in the row with John.

***

When I was little, we lived in Chicago, and Dr. Hess was the minister at Warren Park Presbyterian Church in Cicero, Illinois. We lived in a house on the same property as the church, which the church owned.

When John and I were seven, we moved to Detroit, and Dr. Hess was the minister at Ward United Presbyterian Church. When the church moved from Detroit to the suburbs, Dr. Hess did not want to live in a church manse; he wanted to have his own house. So he worked it out with the church board that he would own his house and they would pay for it. So then he got to keep his house.

The clever, cunning Dr. Hess figured out some things. He bought land a mile down the road, and the board of his church approved this. He did not tell the Presbyterian officials that he had bought the land for himself because normally the church would have owned the land and the house. Then at one point he officially separated from the United Presbyterian Church (UPC) and started the Evangelical Presbyterian Church, taking the land for the new church with him and not telling the UPC. He got away with things like this all the time.

At Christmas, he would have someone from the church come to our house and put up Christmas lights and decorations. He never paid them to do the work, because they were "doing it for the Lord."

Dr. Hess went to the church each morning, and when he came back in the early afternoon he and Mrs. Hess would take a one-mile walk. They would hold arms and talk. When they came back, they would go to separate bedrooms and have a nap. After the nap, Dr. Hess would go to the church to see people.

Sometimes when Dr. and Mrs. Hess would go on their afternoon walk, I would run out and tap Dr. Hess and say, "Got you." He would turn around and run back to the door and tap me and say, "Got you." We would do that for a while. That is the only time he and I related. It really annoyed Mrs. Hess that he was giving me attention. That's why I kept doing it – because it annoyed her so much. It is the only time I existed in their relationship or to him.

Family Dynamics

I was introduced to transactional analysis many years ago, and it helped me to understand my family of origin. There are five different ways that people relate to each other: 1. unconditional love, 2. conditional love, 3. conditional dislike, 4. unconditional dislike, 5. discounting. This last one, discounting, is the worst, and the schizophrenic family usually has a lot of discounting.

In transactional analysis, there's something called the Karpman Triangle. That is the persecutor-rescuer-victim dynamic. Mrs. Hess was constantly in the ultimate victim role. I was the persecutor. My sister Deborah was the rescuer. She agreed with my mother about how awful I was. I believe this dynamic is played out frequently in schizophrenic families and society. I believe that in most normal families where members are living in reality, the game is always played with some degree of ambivalence (at most it is 85 percent to 90 percent the other person's fault). I believe that in psychotic families (like the Hess family), the dynamic is played out as 100 percent the other person's fault. Psychosis is a thinking disorder because there is NO room for the perceived persecutor's needs or existence. The victim believes he or she is 100 percent right. The perceived persecutor does not exist at all or have any needs.

Dan was Dr. Hess' favorite and John did his relating outside of the family. When people in the church spoke about us, Dan was the smart one. Deborah was the sweet one (which she hated and eventually put all her effort into changing that perception). I was the stupid one – that was the only way I existed, by how moronically stupid I was. My older brother Dan had one friend in the church, Clark, who was always getting into trouble doing things that weren't exactly legal. But Dan stood by Clark, laughing and supporting him.

Dan got into some serious trouble when he was at Wheaton College. He called a professor anonymously and threatened him. The college figured out that it was Dan calling and they kicked him out. Dan went to college in Chicago for a while, but he managed to get back into Wheaton before he graduated. It was all covered up – Dr. Hess had to maintain his perfect image in the church.

Recently, Deborah told me a story in a very angry, visceral, guttural, and determined tone of voice (of which she was totally unaware). When she was a freshman and Dan was a senior in high school, she decided that she would be number one and Dan would not be by the end of the school year. And she did it. From then on Deborah became Dr. Hess' favorite and I perceived Dan as broken.

Dr. Hess wanted Dan to be a Presbyterian minister because Dr. Hess was, and so was Dr. Hess' father. There was a huge battle when Dan was in college. He did not want to be a minister. He became a lawyer instead, and it was like he failed miserably in Dr. Hess' eyes. After that, Deborah became even more the favorite in the family.

Dan was compulsive. He wanted to run for office when he grew up, and he kept running for office and losing. He ran for office about 10 times but never won.

My twin John was in the Navy and was sent to Korea, where he met a girl. She got pregnant, and when Dr. and Mrs. Hess found out, they flew to Korea and had John and the girl get married immediately. Then the newlyweds had to live in Grand Rapids, Michigan, until the baby was born so that no one in the church would find out that she was pregnant before they got married.

Intelligence and accomplishments were important in the Hess family. My sister earned a PhD and was the head of a French department at a university. My two brothers became lawyers. I was considered the stupid one. So when I was a young adult I decided to take an IQ test. I didn't tell anyone because I figured I would flunk it and officially prove how stupid I was. But I earned a score 20 points above a genius IQ – wow! It seemed to me they must have given me the wrong test.

At my twin brother's wedding - mimicking others to look "normal"

Him

Him had a large, round body that was filled with heavy, toxic energy. When he came in and covered me up, I became even more disconnected from others and from reality. But Him also saved my life. I was not connected to anyone. I did not relate with anyone. If I had not had Him to relate to, I could not have survived.

I had a dream once, when I was about nine, where I was lying on the bed and Him was covering me. My brothers and sister showed up. Dan, Deborah, and John were standing up, leaning against the wall. They were casually, curiously watching me. At the first opportunity, I begged them as forcefully as I could – by sending my thoughts – to help me get rid of Him. I shot this desperate thought to them, asking them, *Please get Him off. Get Him off so I can come there.*

They were picking up my thoughts and understood everything that was going on for me. They knew what dire straits I was in, but they were bored and did not care at all. They casually stood up and walked out of the room. This was how my relationship with them in real life was. They couldn't have bothered. We didn't have a relationship. When they walked away, Him covered me even more. He became stronger and thicker and separated me from reality even more. He only had this power because humans did not relate to me. If they had related, he would have lost all of his power.

Making Friends

Mrs. Hess was oblivious to everything. I would take money out of her wallet when it was on the dresser. I did it over and over and over and she never knew it. Once, I took money from Dr. Hess' wallet on the same dresser and he knew it instantly. I thought, *Oh boy, don't ever take it from Dr. Hess again.*

Candy kept me alive as a child. I used the money I took from Mrs. Hess to buy candy at the store. I hid the candy under my bed in the room that I shared with my sister Deborah. When Deborah found out about the candy under my bed, she was enraged. She was a diabetic and couldn't have candy. Deborah was vicious to me verbally, although she never talked to me about the candy. But she told Mrs. Hess, who eventually allowed Deborah to move into an upstairs bedroom. Nobody EVER talked to me about this. Mrs. Hess and Deborah were quite entrenched in the Victim-Persecutor-Rescuer triangle. Deborah was the victim, I was the persecutor, and Mrs. Hess was the rescuer. They acted this out frequently and sometimes switched so that Mrs. Hess was the victim and Deborah was the rescuer. I was totally unaware of this dynamic until years later.

I didn't have any friends. In the Hess family, we were not allowed to play with the kids in the neighborhood because Mrs. Hess thought that since they were working class, they would influence us and we would not go to college. I was only in preschool!

So when I was seven, and we lived in Chicago, I worked up the nerve to walk up to a group of girls and ask if they wanted some candy. They were excited and said "yes." So we walked over to the candy store next to the school. There was a big glass counter where all the candy was and a very tall man standing behind the counter. I reached up as high as I could, on my tiptoes, and placed the money on the counter. I asked him to get the girls whatever candy they wanted. He silently looked at me with piercing eyes, then turned to the girls and got them what they asked for. As soon as they had the candy, we left the store and they ran ahead laughing and went off to eat their candy. I was totally forgotten by them and left alone.

When the girls ran away everything settled inside, back into total disconnected, detached nothingness. And it was like, *Okay, that's what I expected. That's what people do.* I wanted to have friends and I tried. But when they ran away right afterward, I thought, *I guess that's not how you make friends.* I didn't try again.

Evidently the clerk called the school because someone my age wasn't supposed to have that amount of money. The next day at school, the first-grade teacher called me up to the desk. I didn't really have feelings, but I was terrified. I knew there was something wrong, even though schizophrenic feelings are not real feelings. Now I was visible and I worked so hard to be invisible to everybody, so they couldn't get me. If I was visible, then I could be annihilated. It was like I was walking to my doom.

She put me on the desk and asked me about the candy. I don't remember what I said. I was afraid to go home that day because I knew I would be in trouble. So after school I went to the house of Lynn and

Lauren, who were twins in my father's church whom John played with.

When I eventually got home, Dr. Hess took me into the room, put me over his knee, pulled my pants down, and spanked me as hard as he could. This just made him all the more terrifying to me. Then he grabbed me, pulled me in, and said, "I did this because I love you." And I thought, *Yeah, that makes sense.* That's what love is to me. It is one of the only times I remember him relating to me, and it was **horrible**.

The Cat

Starting in second grade, I would come home from school and sit on the front steps petting the cat for hours. Mrs. Hess never missed me or came looking for me. That's the first time I remember feeling good feelings from physical contact. Mrs. Hess HATED animals, and we were never allowed to take the cat into the house. It lived in a barrel in the garage. When I was 12, I sneaked the cat into my bedroom so it was more comfortable for me to pet it. I closed the door, but at some point Mrs. Hess discovered what I had done. She went absolutely WILD and screamed at me. She was totally out of control and violently furious with me. I never snuck the cat in again.

I read once that usually there is something wrong with people who don't like animals. This is true in my experience. When I was older, I would keep my room very messy. It bothered Mrs. Hess so she would stay out of my room. It was one way I protected myself and survived. Mrs. Hess was completely emotionally detached. She would yell and scream, but she only hit me maybe once.

Petting cats was the first time I ever felt positive, reciprocal touch.

Deborah

Recently, when I was talking to Deborah about our childhood, I realized that I was not real to her with my own set of needs **at all**. She would never admit this, but I can tell. I did not exist to her as a real person in any kind of a positive way. And this is how everyone in the family treated me. I was not real to anyone at all. All that existed were my mother's and Deborah's needs. The few times I have tried to talk to my sister about my physiological or emotional experience, she has had absolutely no interest in the conversation.

I learned a lot from how out of touch with me Deborah was. It was very informative for me. I eventually learned how to draw emotional conclusions from interactions, which to me felt like a miracle.

Deborah was married and they were both professors – achievement was all that mattered. They had two sons, who each ended up with manic depressive disorder.

She eventually was divorced, and when I asked her about that, she said it was because they both worked "100 hours a week." Obviously, that was not true.

My sister was always number one in the family, especially in academics. The only area that I did better than her was with boys. They weren't very interested in her, and she didn't know how to relate. As a schizophrenic, I would put on a pseudo self when I had to interact with people. I guess I did a pretty darn good job with it because I dated a lot of guys. I always had guys falling all over me. It seemed easy to get them, maybe because I did not want to get serious with them. I used them to try to get into reality. When it did not work with one, I would swap him for another and try again.

My sister was jealous of me because she didn't date much. But on my part, it was all a performance. I tried to get real with each one, talking about what I thought I was supposed to do, and I would do the things that I thought I was meant to do, but it didn't work.

In college, I started having sex because I thought you were supposed to. I never had any sexual feelings because I was always disconnected from my body. When I was having sex, I was most detached. I was on the ceiling watching everything, just knowing how I was supposed to perform. At some point the guy I was dating might want to get more serious, and that did not work for me. So it would end. There were always other guys waiting in line. So I swapped one for the next to see if that would work.

Six Weeks Every Summer

Each summer from the middle of July to the end of August we took a six-week trip, usually in the car. When we started our trip, Mrs. Hess was always driving, and Dr. Hess was in the passenger seat. I never heard my parents fight except at the beginning of our summer trip each year. They would get into the biggest argument where they were just screaming at each other. It was kind of unbelievable. The four of us children just sat in the car, cowering in silence. The argument would last for about 20 minutes and that was it. We children were all in the back seat, quiet and listening to everything. That is the only time I ever heard them fight. It was refreshing, actually – at least they were doing something real and honest.

The goal on these trips was not to relax; the goal was to do lots of stuff. We would go to two or three museums every day. I was bored to tears. I just wandered around looking at things. It was their vacation. We never went to visit family.

One time we went to the Outer Banks of North Carolina, and we were on Ocracoke Island, which was one mile wide and 16 miles long. Dr. Hess went a bit crazy because there was nothing intellectual for him to do. I can't remember exactly what he did. I was not in touch with reality enough to know, but I could feel he was miserable.

I loved it. There was water and sun and sand and nice people. And I didn't have to race, trying to keep up with Dr. and Mrs. Hess, who usually took us to museum after museum.

Dr. Hess liked to take chances. They went to Europe in 1939, just before World War II broke out. They were in Germany and barely made it out on time. He was always doing stuff like that – challenging things – thinking that it proved how clever he was.

***

For our vacation during the summer I was seven, we went on a ship to Europe. I wandered all over the ship all alone. Mrs. Hess was totally oblivious to where I was. I didn't know this wasn't normal.

There was an elevator man on the ship who started talking to me one day. I thought, *That's really strange. Big people don't talk to me. Why are you talking to me? And he's not even talking to the other adults who are next to me.* One day I went to see him on the elevator and he stopped the elevator between two floors and had me pull my skirt up and pull my pants down. He started licking me. My heart sank.

I looked up and there was a shaft of light where the next floor was, and this was where the wise old soul would always show up. I saw that light and I thought, *Will I survive this? Will I live to be up on that floor? I don't know.* But I did exactly what he wanted me to do. The wise old soul told me don't move, don't budge. Let him do whatever he wants, act like you're going along with it, and then when you can, escape. And that's what I did. I kept myself alive. When he was done, he let me out. I never went to the elevator again.

When we were leaving the ship, Mrs. Hess, who never said anything nice to me, said, "Oh, there's your friend, the elevator man. Wave to the elevator man." My heart sank, but I raised my hand and I waved. It never occurred to me to tell anybody about what the man had done, because no one would be interested. It was always up to me to save myself from dire circumstances.

While we were on the ship there was a huge storm, and water was pouring across the bow. I went up to the top of the ship and opened the door to the bow of the ship – I thought that I probably shouldn't be there. Him was there above the ship and over the ocean saying, "Come, join me, we'll have the perfect ending." (He wanted me to kill myself.) And I looked at Him and resolutely shut the door. Him was a toxic being and maybe a lost soul who lived on the earth plane who pushed me to hurt myself. But there was also something inside of me keeping me alive, an ancient wise being, which is a part of me. That being saved me over and over and over, keeping me alive.

PART II

Navigating the World

College

As I finished high school and planned for college, I thought I would go to Wheaton College in Chicago. Everybody in our family went there because it was both Christian and highly academic. Both Dan and Deborah had attended Wheaton. But since I was the *stupid one* in the family – remember, I had earned a D in algebra – Dr. Hess thought I would flunk out of Wheaton, and that would ABSOLUTELY not be acceptable. So I went to Houghton College in New York instead.

Houghton was in a small town in New York, with a population of 250 people. It had strict rules, and we had to be in bed by 10 o'clock. I started out at Houghton as a piano major because I had taken piano lessons from age seven. But then I figured out that I couldn't make much of a living playing the piano. So the next easiest thing in which to major was elementary education. So I did that.

In classes I would sit in the front so there were no people in front of me and I could just watch the teacher. I don't remember relating to anybody. I would mimic and say what I was supposed to, but I never did anything socially with anyone. I spent most of the time in my bedroom.

I found Houghton to be boring, so for my sophomore year I transferred to Wheaton. I thought the reason I got into Wheaton was because they needed students. I think it was a lot easier to get in as a transfer.

I liked philosophy because it seemed like more of a total perspective. When I had to write a paper, it was like I could leap off and just do my own thing. I had a philosophy class and we had to write a creative essay comparing three different philosophers. After I wrote it and turned it in, the professor had me come to the front and read my essay to the whole class. I was positive he wanted to show everyone an example of a poorly written essay. It didn't occur to me until years later that maybe it was the opposite – maybe I was a positive example.

I had different roommates every year. I guess I was strange to other people, but of course since I was out of touch, I was not aware of the other person's experience. When I think back, I have no clue how I got through college, much less how I graduated with honors, because nothing was real to me.

.

Going Abroad

As a child I was taught that traveling to see many places was normal, and so after my sophomore year, I went on a world trip. Wheaton College had summer missionary trips and I applied to work in an orphanage abroad over the summer. Some people went to downtown Chicago, but I was sent to Hong Kong. I discovered that if I paid $140, I could do an around-the-world trip and stop in many places of the 12,000 miles along the way, so I did. First I stopped in Hawaii, then Japan, and then I went to Hong Kong.

I did all this on my own. The Hesses never asked me anything about the trip or where I was going. There was no sense of concern and I wasn't used to saying anything – so I didn't.

I was in Hong Kong working at the orphanage for over two months. The one word I learned was "don-yet sund," which means "just a moment." So that's what I would say to the children.

After two months, I continued on my trip around the world. I thought it would be interesting to go to Vietnam to see what war was like. It was the summer of 1966, during the heaviest part of the Vietnam war. I flew to Saigon and quickly met a missionary who was going to Kaitac (an American military camp outside of Saigon). Tourists were not allowed to leave Saigon at that time because of the war. He asked if I wanted to go as his assistant. I thought that would be an interesting adventure, so I said "yes" and went with him to the camp. I was not in reality, so I had no sense of danger.

While we were there, during the night, the Vietcong bombed the camp, and we had to run to dirt holes to protect ourselves. In the middle of the bombing, a vague thought occurred to me: *Maybe this wasn't such a good idea.* Then I thought, *It'll be fine.*

The next day the camp director found out that I was not really an official assistant and he had two soldiers drive me back to Saigon. We were in an open jeep, and at one point there was a bus stopped on the road going the other direction. The soldiers ground to a halt, picked up their rifles, cocked them, and pointed them right at the bus. Once again, I had a fleeting thought: *Maybe this wasn't such a good idea.*

The bus slowly pulled away while the soldiers kept their guns pointed at it. After the bus was gone, the soldiers told me that a week earlier the Vietcong had been hiding behind a bus and shot some soldiers in the back, killing them.

Next I flew to Thailand, and then I went to all the USSR satellite countries. I could not go to the Soviet Union since I had not planned ahead. The people seemed nice but a lot more subdued. Very few Americans visited this part of the world – behind the Iron Curtain in the 1960s – and I did not meet any other Americans while I was there.

After that, I went to Norway, Sweden, Denmark, and Iceland. I traveled to a total of 32 countries, all by myself, on this four-month trip. It would've been much harder to have someone with me because I would have had to pretend.

Many people would have been interested in the cultures that I visited. But none of it was real to me as a schizophrenic who was not living in reality. I am sure if

I went back there now, with my new awareness of reality, I would be totally engrossed in the various nuances of culture. But at the time, none of that was real to me.

One thing did stand out for me, and that was the Taj Mahal in India. As soon as I arrived in India, even though it was night, I hired a taxi to take me to the iconic monument. The Taj Mahal at night in the moonlight is the most beautiful building I have ever seen. The side of the building is covered in intricate figures made with small stones in orange and yellow and many other colors. It was absolutely breathtaking.

Nepal was my favorite country. The only way to get there was to fly over the Himalayan mountains. When we landed, it was like we were in a sacred space. When I was walking around Kathmandu, I passed by a church and I started looking at the decorations on the church. As I looked closer and closer I realized that all the decorations were of sexual positions. I couldn't believe it. I guess that was part of their culture or religion.

In Kathmandu, I met a very friendly person who offered to take me into his home. It was a wooden home, and on the first floor of the house were all of the animals – cows, goats, and sheep. The living area was upstairs. It was very unusual, but also peaceful and quiet.

Tibet was north of Nepal, but I couldn't go there because it was part of Communist China.

I had another interesting experience when I was flying home. I had run out of money, so I just survived on the meals given out on the flights. When I mentioned it to the man next to me on one of the flights, he stood up and asked for anyone on the plane who had not eaten their lunch to pass it back to me. I was shocked! I had no idea people did things like that for each other.

When I landed back in Detroit, I called up the Hesses and asked if they could pick me up at the airport. They said that they were too busy and told me to take a taxi home, so I did. When I arrived, no one asked me anything about my trip around the world. Now that I'm in touch with reality, I realize that this is pretty abnormal. It didn't occur to me at the time or for decades after. But now that I am more in reality, it's hard to believe that they did not pick me up at the airport and never asked anything about my travels.

Even when I told them that I had gone to Vietnam, in the middle of a war, they weren't concerned at all.

I took about 3,000 slides on the trip. An interesting note is that all the photos I took were of places without people in them. People were not real to me. I later realized that this was a result of my failure to bond with humans and my need to cathect to objects around me to create my own womb. This is common for schizophrenics. Just look at schizophrenics on the streets and their grocery carts overflowing with stuff.

I brought the photos home in a bag and put them on the shelf in the garage. Shortly after I got home, Mrs. Hess cleaned out the garage and threw out all my pictures, without ever asking me or looking at them. When I said that I was upset, it didn't faze her at all. She was just irritated that I was upset with her. She had no sense of what it meant for her to throw out all the pictures from my trip around the world. Dr. Hess always took tons of pictures on trips and they were all saved. Why would she treat my slides so totally differently without any awareness? I just didn't get it.

The Cuckoo's Nest

I realize now that I spent my whole life looking for my real self, even though I was not aware that that was what I was doing. I looked okay and sounded okay, but I had no connection to anyone. Finding myself and getting into reality was a long process.

There was, as far back as I can remember, this drive to kill myself. That is one of the things that Him encouraged me to do. I am not sure if having suicidal thoughts is why I decided to see a therapist when I was at Wheaton, but it likely was the reason. During my senior year I saw a therapist for traditional talk therapy and it did not do a thing for me.

I had learned to act as if I was fine, but I knew that if I kept looking okay I would not get the help that I needed. At one point I had a session with Dr. Esau, the top psychiatrist in the practice, so I let my real crazy self come out, which I had worked so hard to cover up for all those years. This involved yelling and being upset and flailing my body. It looked like a disintegration – like a total meltdown. But it was just me letting it all out.

When Dr. Esau saw what was happening, he put me in a psychiatric hospital. It was such a relief. It was the first time in my life that I felt like I was where I belonged. That was the first time my outside ever matched my inside. The environment met me where I was. Before that I had to pretend to be someone else to survive. I had observed the mood of others, with detachment, for survival. Everything had been with the purpose of not being killed or annihilated. It was survival, but it was not feeling. It was all an act. Being in the hospital, it was a tremendous relief to no longer have to pretend but rather to begin to learn how to be real.

It was the first time in my life that I felt safe. I would watch the locked door for hours, seeing people going in and out of the door to the hospital. I was so relieved that I wasn't allowed to go out the door. The locked door meant that I could not act on the destructive thought that I had. I was safe in the hospital. I could not hurt myself.

The movie *One Flew Over the Cuckoo's Nest* came out right at the time that I was hospitalized. The movie perfectly portrays the nurse who was in charge of me while I was in the hospital.

In college, I had a white teddy bear that I slept with. When they put me in the hospital, they took my teddy bear and put it up on a shelf behind the nurse's desk. I would come to the desk and stand there for a long time just looking at my teddy bear, wishing that I could have it. I cannot remember if I asked for it; I was not in reality enough to remember that. They may have taken the bear away so that I would attach to Mrs. Hess instead of an object. But Mrs. Hess refused to stay in the hospital with me. She was once again the ultimate victim.

Dr. Esau worked with me for the four months that I was in the hospital. He met me at my level and did regressive reparenting work with me. This was the first time I ever had any real contact with someone in reality. Dr. Esau even included my parents. They would come every two weeks for a session with me. They were in Detroit and had to travel to Chicago for the sessions.

When I returned home, Dr. Esau suggested that Mrs. Hess sleep in the same room with me to help me bond in the reparenting process. She would be in one twin bed and I would be in the other. She did and it was the first time I felt cared for by Mrs. Hess.

Recently, Deborah expressed shock and disgust that Dr. Esau had them come for the sessions with me and suggested that Mrs. Hess sleep in the room with me. Once again I didn't exist to Deborah on any level, either as being my own autonomous self or having any of my own needs. Now I understand that Dr. and Mrs. Hess' needs existed to Deborah but mine did not exist to her at all. This was never real to me until fairly recently. Being in reality now is like an incredible miracle. Even supposedly "bad" feelings like sadness or emotional pain are phenomenally stunning and wonderful.

Schizophrenia is definitely a thinking disorder because no one relates to you as an autonomous person with real needs. What helps me the MOST to be in reality is experiencing objective, true emotional facts. In a schizophrenogenic family, the designated crazy one has no existence or emotional needs on any level whatsoever.

Working as a Secretary

One day as I was driving – after I had graduated from Wheaton College – I saw homeless people along the road, and I absolutely, totally thought that's how I would end up – as a homeless person. At that point I was living at the Hesses' because there was no way I could have lived on my own. I have since found someone else to help take care of me – my wonderful Christopher, who I will talk about later.

In the Hess family system, advanced degrees were absolutely expected. So I applied to the University of Michigan for a master's degree. I had experienced therapy and so I chose social work. I was accepted and was given a scholarship – but there was no way I could do social work because it was all about relationships and I had no clue how to relate. I was not in reality, and I knew I could not produce what was needed.

So, I decided to try being a secretary, and I discovered that I was really, really good at it. I would work four times as much as everyone else and be paid the same amount. Everyone wanted to hire me. But after a few months, I couldn't be around people anymore. So I would quit.

Then I thought of working temporary jobs and it was perfect. Each time, after two or three months when the position ended, I would take a break because I needed to retreat and regroup. I could not keep up with the pseudo-relating anymore. And that way I did not have to look bad when I quit the job. All that ever mattered to the Hesses was producing and looking good.

While I was a secretary a new thing called zip codes came out. To mail something, you now needed the correct zip code – so books were created with all addresses and the correct zip code, which everyone now needed. The books cost $1.00, and I found out I was a born salesperson – because when you're selling something, you need to really believe it will help the people who are buying it and I did. I spent two hours in the evenings selling zip code books and made twice as much money as I had working eight hours as a secretary.

Carrying the Mail

One day I saw a letter carrier and I thought, *That looks like fun.* I applied to work as a letter carrier and they told me there was a six-month waiting list. I thought I would get a nice break. I took a test that was four hours long and very difficult. I was surprised when they called me two weeks later and said I would begin working right away – I had earned a 100 percent on the test! After growing up in the Hess house, nothing makes me believe I'm smart. I thought maybe they had given me the wrong test. But now I am working on believing that I am smart because earning 100 percent on a government test does not generally happen if you are stupid.

So at age 27, I became a letter carrier. Working as a letter carrier was the perfect job for me. I was outside, walking, and alone. I didn't have to interact with people. It was very routine – the same thing over and over – and predictable. The repetition, structure, and consistency were absolutely crucial for me. It was like playing the whole time. I had one of the longest routes and I would always get back on time. I made it a game to see how quickly I could do it! I would try new things that would make the route more efficient and take less time. If I didn't want to talk to someone, I could always say, "I'm late so I have to get going." I was a letter carrier for 41 1/2 years.

There were many guys who wanted to date me at this time. I guess I was a bit of a looker back then. Yeah. There was one guy whom I dated who really liked me, but he had some problems. So I encouraged him to go to therapy because I had gone and he did. One night we were watching TV and I felt an emotional shift in him that meant he was growing. I was panic-stricken because I was not growing like that at all.

Then one day he told me that he wanted to get married and have a family. I knew that I could not do that! Suggesting he go to therapy did not quite work out the way I thought it would; so I've never encouraged anyone else to go to therapy again – which I feel kind of guilty about.

Him, In Adulthood

Him kept me alive growing up because I had someone to relate to. However, Him also encouraged me to kill myself on a regular basis. When I was a child we took a trip to the Empire State Building. I remember wanting to climb up the fence and jump over from the top of the building. But I did not act on this thought no matter how tempted I was. I never told anyone about this. It never occurred to me to talk to anyone about it.

Him totally covered me up – and that's one main reason why I couldn't feel anything in reality. It was a tortuous relationship since he was constantly encouraging me to kill myself. But I would not have survived if I had not had Him.

Years later, I worked with Sandy Landsman, who did regressive therapy to reparent schizophrenics. It was the first time that anyone ever tried to help me with Him. We were at a weekend workshop and we went outside.

Him was in the tree and everyone sent all their energy to push him away. This was huge. No one had ever believed that Him was real, and I certainly never had anyone do anything about Him. This event didn't get rid of Him, but it was the first time that people ever tried to help me send Him away. It was unbelievable to have this support and help. For the first time ever I existed as a real person.

Christopher

In my late 20s I met Christopher, a fellow letter carrier. He would end up as the most important man in my life – even to this day. He worked in a different section and he was a very generous, supportive, caring person. He felt safe to me. He had a college degree and was very smart, but he had no one to really guide him. Neither of his parents had gone to college.

Christopher is a wonderful person, but he has a lot of anxiety. He went to a private Catholic boys high school and never dated anyone. Both of his parents were alcoholics. His mother died when he was 12 of cirrhosis of the liver. His father was a high-level manager at the post office. He had asked Christopher if it was okay if he kept working afternoons, which would mean that Christopher would be home alone after school. Christopher said *yes*. So he was on his own after that.

When Christopher graduated from college, he became a letter carrier. He hated it even though he was very good at it. He just didn't know what else to do. Because of his excellent performance, he was offered a supervisor position – but he didn't want to be a supervisor. With his skill set he would have been fantastic working with computers. He did not have anyone to guide him, and this showed me how important mentoring is.

The first time we went out on a date, he brought a stuffed teddy bear for me. It was like he knew who I was in the essence of my being. It was unbelievable, and I was really overwhelmed by the gift. I named the bear Myron and I loved holding him. It was like Myron and I belonged together. And it's been like that ever since.

Christopher and I spent a lot of time together. One night I began kissing him because that's what I thought I was supposed to do. He didn't respond at all at first, and then he kind of woke up and responded to me. It shocked me and I stopped immediately – I have never started anything romantic since. It's never been sexual between us, which has been perfect for me.

Eventually we created a pattern where he took care of me. He was kind, accepting, and generous. I suppose looking back on it, I supplied him with a form of companionship, even though I was quite young emotionally. While Him was still operating in my life, I had now gained a person in the real world who would become my pseudo-parent. I could not have stayed alive without him. He offered me a home and monetary support and took care of my physical well-being. As generous as this all was, I still was not in reality. It would take many years and many therapists before I would find the reparenting that I needed.

PART III

Growing Into Reality

Since I was a senior in college, my whole job has been to retrieve my real self and grow into me. So sometimes now I'll say to God, with a big grin on my face, "So God, how am I doing on my assignment now?"

I found solace in my cat named Boots.

Therapists

I've been in therapy since my junior year of college. The only therapies that helped me were those that did not use traditional methods. For a therapist to help me, they had to be willing to function outside the box. They also needed to trust me and to believe me when I would tell them what I needed. For instance, many times I needed to be held like a baby and be given a bottle.

I saw many, many therapists as I was constantly looking for those who were willing and able to help me. I do not remember them all – especially the ones who were traditional. (I called them PH heads, which stands for professional heads, because they were the rule followers.) I tend to remember the ones who actually helped me. But since I was not in reality, my memory is not necessarily chronological. Different therapists had different pieces of the puzzle that eventually helped me come into reality. Here they are:

Sandy Landsman

Sandy Landsman did regressive therapy with schizophrenics and ran a reparenting group. She was the only therapist in the area who was trained in reparenting. She had trained with Jaqui Schiff, a therapist who followed the model proposed by the author of *Reparenting Schizophrenics: The Cathexis Experience* by Elaine Childs-Gowell. Sandy was brilliant and very committed. The reparenting group was fantastic for me. It was made up of other schizophrenics and clients of Sandy.

One of the things that we did was rage reduction. We would all lie on the floor (I would be flat on my back), and the rest of the group would hold a part of my body. Then I was to rage and scream and throw my body around. This made me feel real for the first time – ever. It was the only thing that was enough to deal with my level of rage. My rage was given permission to be.

Sandy used parenting techniques for children with us. She was explicit in her instructions and had clear structure with all of us. I started to exist for the first time ever because someone was meeting me where I was. As I mentioned earlier, Sandy was the first person who ever helped me address Him. It was crucial that she believed he was real.

After five years, Sandy moved to Florida. So I would travel to see her in Florida every six weeks and spend a weekend with her to continue reparenting therapy. Christopher paid for my plane tickets. That was so huge because he was taking charge – he was functioning as a parent, which is what I needed.

After about a year, Sandy casually told me, in front of a group, that I had done all the therapy I needed to do and she was done working with me, which was devastating. She had discounted where I was *and* had dumped me, which was my constant fear.

Kathleen

In Sandy Landsman's group I met a woman named Kathleen, who became a crucial support for me for most of my life. I was 28 when I met her. She happened to be a therapist, but we developed a friendship, not a therapist-client relationship. This was unusual as I was not really capable of having friends. She was always there for me. As I became more integrated, she introduced me to a lot of things that were happening in the world. Through all that time, she was always available to me without expecting anything in return. Strangely enough, the worse shape I was in, the more she was there for me.

Kathleen enjoyed doing the reparenting work that I like to call my *little* work. For years, Kathleen took care of me as one would a baby or small child. She would hold me, feed me a bottle, read me a story, and wash my hair – all the things that parents would do for a little one. I do not think that I could have made it without her since she gave me so much time to be little. This helped me grow.

Kathleen had a problem with getting to places on time or at all. So I would either meet her at her house or she would come to mine. That way, at her house, she'd always be there, or at my home I could do whatever until she arrived.

Elizabeth Alberta

The next significant therapist I worked with was Elizabeth, who was a profound help to me. She was a nontraditional therapist doing energy work (soul retrieval, regressive therapy, Reiki, etc.). Elizabeth was willing to meet me right where I was, and she literally brought my real self out of the inky black space of nothingness. She guided me to access the memory of when I received my assignment from God. Working with her enabled me to remember my origin story that I shared in the beginning of the book where I saw the Hesses before I was born.

Elizabeth also did reparenting work with me (at the baby stage) and introduced me to energy work, which helped me begin to feel my body. Before that, I had never existed in my body. I worked actively with her for many years, and I occasionally still see her; and although she is retired, I also speak to her on the phone every few weeks. I appreciate still having her in my life since she has known me for over 30 years. She tells me regularly how brilliant I am. I have a hard time taking this in because of the messages that I received from the

Hesses in my childhood. But it helps that Elizabeth tells me that she has never seen anyone change as much as I have. Maybe someday I will change enough to believe that I am a genius like she keeps telling me.

I did some work with a female therapist in Grosse Pointe, Michigan, who did nontraditional therapy with me. She worked with me in reparenting and regressive work as well as sessions in the hot tub (representing the womb). I saw her for several years until she moved out of state. She was similar to the various nontraditional therapists I saw during these years who did reparenting through tub work and tried to have me attach as a baby would.

Dr. Sack

I met Dr. Sack, a psychiatrist and family care provider, through Kathleen, who was a patient of his. I started seeing him also, and I have for the last 30 years. He prescribes my psychiatric medications, many of which have not had any effect. The one medication that has been helpful is my sleep medication, which helps me sleep and feel rested and has been vital to my recovery. It is both a sleep and an antipsychotic medication, and I take a very high dose. It is important for patients to work with medical professionals to find what works best for them and their situation. It can take years to find the best fit.

It is important to note that the usual way doctors treat schizophrenia is with medications. In my experience, the medications for schizophrenia have been created to mask the symptoms of schizophrenia to make those around them more comfortable. They did not help me at all.

Steve Campbell

Steve Campbell took over Sandy's group for schizophrenics. I remember working with him, and he would have us sit on the floor. It was fantastic because it broke the PH head rules. I would sing solo sometimes – one time I even sang to him, but I couldn't face him while I sang, so I stood up and turned my back to him. When I turned around he had tears streaming down his face. I was just so shocked because I was not used to people responding to me like that.

Steve couldn't get through to me, and yet he was very aware of how gone I was. He was obviously an out-of-the-box therapist. Steve wrote the amazing poem for me that is at the beginning of the book. When he wrote this poem it wasn't real to me at all. Now, when I read the poem, I am amazed he knew all this about me – now it is all real to me. Steve worked with me for almost a decade before he died.

Shirana Joy

Up to this point I went by the name that the Hesses had given me, which was Janet. But that name felt cold and dead, not at all like me. Sometime in the 1980s, I was in a spiritual workshop and we broke into groups of about four people. I was sitting on the floor with this group and the name Shirana came to me as if it was my soul name! So I started using it as my name. I later added Joy because that is my goal in life – both to experience joy and to create joy.

Christine Elwart

From the first moment that I met Chris, in the late 1980s, I knew that she was incredibly special and I needed to work with her. I had never had this experience before. But she was so busy that I was told that I could see her for only six sessions. I did not know what I was going to do, but I knew that I had to make it work. After the fifth session, she suggested that I work with her husband, Joe, who was also a therapist. And my heart leapt for joy because that meant I could have more than six sessions. I knew that Chris was a key for me in order to experience reality. And it has proven to be absolutely true. She has become my mom – my one and only real mom. Chris was one of the rare individuals who was willing to learn from and with me. It would never have worked otherwise.

Chris: Shirana shared with me the principles of reparenting and how it affected her up to that point. This was a whole new approach that I was not familiar with, but I intuitively knew this was the path to pursue. I had a pretty steep learning curve, and I read everything I could on the topic, including the book Reparenting Schizophrenics *(upon which much of Sandy Landsman and Steve Campbell's work was based). They primarily worked with Shirana in a group setting, with some supporting one-on-one work. Most of my work with Shirana was individual, although there were several years in which Shirana was part of a group with Joe and me.*

My work with Shirana was completely unconventional and outside the box. Shirana knew what she needed, and I trusted her to know and to tell me what that was. Shirana told me that she had no real self and that she was about the business of growing her child from the womb experience on. This required me to suspend many of the things that I had learned before as a therapist, and to meet her where she was. It was a challenging and exhilarating journey. I often had no template on which to depend and no modality that fit her circumstances. Together we created a new roadmap to reality as well as a new path of treatment for schizophrenics.

Chris helped me to grow a healthy parent inside of me. Before this, therapists had told me to nurture myself. But that was never real to me. All that suggestion did was to send me off into my own world, where I was totally disconnected. As a schizophrenic I did not have a healthy adult, parent, or child inside of me.

But with Chris' help, I have grown to where we are starting to see a real parent, a real adult, and a healthy child inside of me. All three of these are growing. I'm learning a lot and gaining healthy emotional tools. The healthy parent that I am growing is beginning to be able to take care of my inner child.

Joe Elwart

Chris: When I considered the daunting task of reparenting, I knew that it would best serve Shirana, to not only have a mom but also a dad as well. When I approached Joe Elwart, who was my husband at the time, he was excited about the prospect.

There was a certain familiarity in working with Joe. He could understand things about me that no one else could. It wasn't until later that I realized that he too came from a schizophrenogenic family. I have a nonverbal, preverbal, kinesthetic experience when I interact with him, which I realize comes from our similar family backgrounds. It is especially helpful to confirm that the problems in my childhood, and within my family of origin, were not 100 percent from me. This is why they call schizophrenia a thinking disorder. One thing about schizophrenia is that it is paralogical – it sounds logical, but it only makes sense to the one thinking it. And when I am in that place, I am 100 percent positive that I am completely right. And Joe got that.

Joe became my dad, and that was crucial. He was much healthier than the Hesses and could understand me. He would sit next to me and let me sit on the floor whenever I needed. It allowed me to exist wherever I was emotionally, which was very young. He accepted me where I was, and he has devoted decades to being my dad.

I could never have come into reality if I had not been accepted by both Chris and Joe – completely – exactly where I was age-wise. When I had to figure it all out by myself, I was racing to do so. But with the support and help of my mom and dad, I was able to slow down because I didn't have to figure everything out all by myself. So in a real way I have been going through childhood for the first time – a healthy childhood.

New Joe

The latest therapist I worked with was "New Joe" (NJ), who has since died. He was what I called a PH head, meaning that he stuck to the rules, which was not optimal for me. I don't think he fully bought into my schizophrenic diagnosis, but I kept going to him because I had a need to report my experiences to a variety of people, creating a therapeutic support network. I had a great need for reality testing, and he provided that. I saw him for about 10 years from 2012 to 2022.

Living with Christopher

Decades ago, I was living in a co-op, but I would spend most of the time staying overnight with Christopher, sleeping on his couch. The rules of the co-op said that I had to spend a certain number of nights there. But clearly I could not live alone. Someone reported that I wasn't there enough, and eventually they kicked me out. So then I moved in with Christopher. I don't know how I could have ever lived alone – I don't know if I could have made it.

I lived in Christopher's house and he took care of me for over 30 years. We were never sexual. I wanted my relationship with him to be real, and if it had been sexual, it would not have been real for me.

Christopher was taught to take care of everybody. In the last two years, I worked on trying to take care of him too. I was able to be soft and supportive and giving, and I kept debating about how much to do for him and how much he needed to do for himself.

I started this new thing about a year ago. I got the idea to have evening snuggle time. At six o'clock every night we sat on the couch and snuggled. And it was wonderful for both of us. It was not sexual at all. It was just nurturing.

I am sad to report that during the writing of this book, Christopher unexpectedly died. I feel sad and lonely, but they are real feelings and that is growth.

The house I shared with Christopher was pretty full of stuff. Christopher asked me to clean stuff out and it was totally legitimate. But I didn't seem to be able to do it. One issue that schizophrenics often have is a tendency to hoard things. I believe that schizophrenics gather lots of objects around them because they never attached to the mother in the womb. Bonding is critical for survival. Instead of bonding with people, we become very attached to the stuff around us. I felt safe with lots of objects around me, like I was in a womb. Also, objects are safer than people; I don't have to worry about objects screaming at me – they are just there.

This is basically what a parent is supposed to do with a baby – just hold them and be there. Objects feel like a soft cushion. It is like a little baby with toys, and love is surrounding them. It felt like my protection, and I felt safer. It also kept Mrs. Hess out of my room.

After a lifetime of collecting stuff, I have saved a lot and now would like to work my way out of that. My bedroom was the worst, and I get why Christpher wanted me to clean it out. But so far I haven't been able to do it. For one thing this is the first time in my life I've been able to have time of my own in reality to do whatever I want, like read. When it comes to choosing to read or clean, it's hard to make myself clean.

My plan to help me is to take pictures of everything in my bedroom and in the house and show my mom and dad. That will allow me to shine the light of day on the dark, hidden parts of me. We will start from exactly where I am as a five-year-old and work our way through it gradually.

Saying Goodbye to Him

Him made it impossible for me to touch reality. In my late forties, Chris, Joe, and I did a Shamanic sweat lodge ceremony to send Him back to the light. Even though he tormented me, he also saved my life; so I wouldn't have been able to let Him go unless we sent him back into the light. I was afraid he would just die otherwise. I remember Him leaving my body and going off to the light. From that moment on, it's like I didn't have this huge cover on me anymore. I was still not in reality, but I could put pieces of me in the right place. I was not covered up and blocked anymore. I was able to start making some real progress. The first step was that I had to attach to real people, so I attached myself to my new mom and dad, Chris and Joe. I could never have made it without them.

Safety in the Car

Being in a car is one of the few places where I felt safe. When I drove in the car, it felt like a protective cocoon. Driving away from people who were dangerous to me helped create even more feelings of safety. Because I felt safe, I would fall asleep when I was driving. I would verbally say to myself, "Don't fall asleep. It's extremely dangerous to do." But it wasn't real to me, no matter what I did. I had many accidents when I fell asleep. I totaled a car when I drove off the side of the road. I can't believe I was never physically injured. God must have been watching out for me.

One time I was on the expressway and I woke up as I was heading down a 40-foot hill, through a stream, and up the other side. I went through a fence, missed a huge tree, and ended up on the eighth hole of the golf course. But nothing happened to my body – I was fine.

When the police came, one of them kept shaking his head, saying, "You're going to church tomorrow, right?" He couldn't believe that I wasn't injured at all. Things like that kept happening to me. Danger wasn't real. I probably totaled about eight cars. It never occurred to me to stop driving because I was not in reality. The last car I had was the first car I did not total. I thought, *I'm gonna see how long cars can last if you don't wreck 'em.*

Sometimes I drive too aggressively. That's what Dr. Hess did all the time – it showed how clever and cunning one was. My identity was tied to being clever and cunning – at least that's what I was taught. When I would drive carefully, it felt kind of blah and boring, so I would speed up to feel. But that was dangerous. So now I'm teaching myself to slow down. If I slow down, some of the energy that went into taking those chances might become available to grow in a healthy way. That's what I'm trusting.

When I was in my forties, Dr. Hess bought me a car. It was the only one he ever bought me. Debbie was number one in the family among the four children (because of her academic success), and so Dr. Hess bought her a car every few years. He never did it for me, but at a certain point I think he must have felt a little guilty and he offered to buy me a car too. I was excited and became a little carried away, and so he set a $12,000 maximum. I chose a Toyota Celica GT-S, bright red. It was wonderful. And that was my favorite car. He never offered to buy me a car again. But I had that car for a long time.

I am a better driver, but still not the best. Just the other day I ran onto the curb and messed up the wheels. I was looking down and didn't realize the road was curved when I smacked my wheel into the curb. It was completely wrecked. I have the general framework of reality, but there are still some holes – it's kind of like Swiss cheese. Thankfully, my mom gives me advice to help me, and I am trying to trust her more.

Dr. and Mrs. Hess

Dr. Hess died in December 1999. When I found out, I did not feel anything. I thought, *Wow, that's interesting. Dr. Hess is not around anymore.* After a short while, I felt relief and the relief kept growing. For the first time in my life I was free to grow a real self. As each member of the Hess family died, it was an abstract fact that was interesting, and then I felt more relief.

After Dr. Hess died, I was integrated enough to know that Mrs. Hess needed help. None of my siblings did anything for her at all. She lived in an assisted living community, and I orchestrated everyone coming in to take care of her. But I did not do it for her because she was my mother – just as a woman who needed help. Mrs. Hess died in 2008. When she died I had this peaceful, white-light feeling inside me that I had done something very sacred in taking care of her. I had never experienced that before. Mrs. Hess never said anything to me about my care, but she did leave me a lump sum of money. I guess this was her way of acknowledging what I had done.

When my twin was diagnosed with myelodysplastic syndrome, I started researching the condition. He needed a bone marrow transplant, and as his twin I was a perfect match for this. I would have given this if he had wanted it, but he was nonverbally adamant about not receiving anything from me. He eventually died from this syndrome.

All but one member of my immediate family are now dead, and it's a relief. I don't have to keep trying to interact with them and make sense of my life. I always blamed myself that I wasn't in touch with reality, but now that I am, I can feel what was missing so drastically in my life.

Becoming Aware
of Others

I was never aware of others before, when I was not in reality. But in the last year I have become aware of what others might need. It is a miracle to be in reality.

I have a sweatshirt that I love to wear. On the back it says: "Dear Person behind me, The world is a better place with you in it." One day when I was wearing the sweatshirt, a woman behind me tapped me on the shoulder. I turned around and she was beaming and filled with white light. I showed her the front, which said: *You are enough.*

I said, "That's what life is all about: passing it forward." And she agreed and told me to have a blessed day. I love it when someone says that. So now I say it. "Have a blessed day!"

Now I am always looking for ways to lift others up in a real and genuine way. I was in a doctor's office and the woman behind the desk had long, brown, flowing hair with a slight curl at the end. I looked her in the eye and told her that her hair was beautiful. She beamed and thanked me. The great thing is that when I lift others up, I feel good too. This is my life now.

Now that I am aware of others, and I have safe people in my life, I am also learning how to ask for help. For most of my life, I was alone and had to figure things out for myself. I have reached the age of about five and am integrated enough that I can actually ask for help and take it in. This is a whole new experience. I am learning that it is okay to trust and depend on someone else. My mom and dad are really specific when they tell me how to do something. Nobody ever did that with me before. This is the first time in my life that this would even work. They say things simply on a five-year-old level. I never felt anything in real life like that when I was growing up. I find that I have to go through each age for the first time in order to grow. Every stage is brand new and emotionally real to me. I am growing up for the first time ever.

Experiencing Emotions

Now, for the first time, coming into reality has opened up the world of emotions for me. For example, a neurotic[1] has an emotional disorder, while a psychotic has a thinking disorder and is not in touch with reality. While I have dealt with psychosis, I have not dealt with neurosis, which is like a foreign language to me. Many of the therapists I worked with treated me in the traditional way with which neurotics are treated. It did not work because first I had to grow my real self before that kind of therapy would have any effect.

When Dr. Esau put me in the hospital, where I belonged, the long process of growing the real me and coming into reality began. Many years later, as my real self grew, I became more in touch with real emotions.

---

1 A personality trait that describes a tendency to experience anxiety, negatively and self-doubt. It is characterized by a long-term tendency to feel negative or anxious.

I learned to experience each emotion as well as to nurture it and help it grow. At first, because they were new to me, I thought that I had to follow each one, because it was real. I had worked so hard to feel emotions, I thought each one was terrific. But I learned that I had to use thinking along with my emotions to know how to take healthy actions.

I had a new experience of emotion this week. Elizabeth (with whom I have a deep and profound relationship) and I agreed that I would write down stuff for the book for 15 minutes every day; then we were to talk about it at three o'clock. I was invested in this, but I wasn't able to do it. It was beyond where I was. I realized that I had never been emotionally connected like that.

One day she did not call and I was hurt. I felt myself emotionally pull back, which I had never, ever done before. I realized that I was protecting myself because I felt hurt that she didn't do what she said she would. I felt that emotion inside of me because I was starting to get more into reality. The next time we talked I felt sort of guilty and I told her about it. She said that what I felt and did was normal. She also said that she had

Covid and that made her not remember things sometimes – that is why she had not called. It was a whole new experience for me.

Building a Foundation

I am learning how to follow directions and to trust my mom and dad in reality. As I keep growing I work on different areas in my life. For a few months now, I've been taking a walk every day to this one big tree – I've lost 74 pounds from walking. The other day I felt like going farther. I had never felt that before, so I did. The next day I decided I wanted to try walking even farther, but I started feeling weighed down. I ran into my old ambivalence. It felt like I did not have a real self to figure out what to do. I was frozen and couldn't decide anything, and I realized I needed my parents to give me structure and tell me how far to go each day. I didn't know how to decide anything; but if they would pick, then I could attach to that.

So I had my mom make a list for the week and write how far to go each day. I put it in my purse and every day I would pull out the list and I would do what the card said to do. I just stayed attached to my mom and followed her instructions on the card – that's been working really well.

It was never safe to be in reality when I was growing up. People around me were not safe, so I had to "race" internally as fast as I could or they might kill me. Before I was in reality, I would fly unbelievably fast along this totally barren land, three feet above the ground with absolutely no one around. I looked down way off in the distance where there were heads with their backs toward me, all facing another direction. They were people in the real world. But I wasn't there at all.

The first time I ever started to exist happened when I was doing this past-life work with Elizabeth in Ann Arbor, Michigan. She was the first one who ever saw the real me as fragmented in inky-black outer space. Elizabeth pulled the scattered parts of me together and put them into my body. This was called soul retrieval. That's the first time I remember having a real me. They say schizophrenics aren't curable – not by traditional methods. It was only therapy that was totally outside of the norm that worked for me.

And now with wonderful people in my life, I know it's safe to be here. This whole process of getting into reality and building a solid foundation has been a methodical, determined work of slowing my insides down – physically, emotionally, intellectually. As I get more and more in touch with reality and my real feelings with real people, my insides slow down more and more.

As I was coming into reality, sometimes I would start to split and disintegrate. When this happened, I would slow down. It was a very precise thing. And if I started to slip and lose it, then I would just sit there and say, *Okay, just go slow, be slow, be right here.* Once I had a past, present, and future, if I started to lose contact with reality, I slowed down and concentrated on the present moment so that I stayed.

Now it feels like when I am in a growth period, my subconscious and unconscious expand and there is more of a solid, real self with which to be in reality. The base is stronger and larger. But sometimes I am discouraged because it is not nearly as exhilarating as the brand new experience of coming out of psychosis was for me.

Navigating Reality

As amazing as it is to finally be in reality, there are many new things to navigate, one of which is ambivalence. When you are crazy, you are 100 percent correct. But reality is more complex. As a schizophrenic I was like a detached brain with pseudo-intellectual thoughts – but they were not real. But internally, there was an absolute belief that I was right. Now that I am in reality, I believe I am right about 85 percent of the time because I am in touch with what is actually happening – and there's room for other possibilities. That is what being in reality feels like.

When I became more in touch with the outside of my body, I wanted it to feel good. I discovered an online clothing store and I went a little crazy buying new clothes. I pushed the button way too many times. Now I have to deal with the consequences of that. There are a lot more complexities out there, all of which I am trying to learn. I am taking myself from where I am right now and learning from my experiences, giving myself reality checks. Sometimes I feel like I am failing, but then someone reminds me that I am just experiencing life.

Now I like to explore the world as a scientist would. In the Hess family, there were absolute rules that existed, but no one ever talked to me about them. But if I broke them, heaven help me. So now that I'm in touch with reality, if something is said to me, I feel real enough inside to ask a question about it and check it out, and that makes it more real. Acting as a scientist – asking questions, using numbers – is one way I stay in touch with reality. When I hear about an action people might take, I then ask: *What percent of people do this? And what percent don't do that?* That helps me stay in touch with reality, even though it often throws the other person off. It really is the most important question I can ask because the numbers allow me to build a grid of external, emotional reality. I am out here in the real world with a pristine canvas.

Right now, I am in reality most of the time. Just a few weeks ago it shifted – again. The most important thing in order for me to stay in reality fully, 100 percent of the time, is to be accepted exactly as I am, where I am, and to share the parts of me that are still crazy.

Developing a Subconscious[1] and an Unconscious[2]

In my experience, schizophrenics are split vertically: One part is a pseudo-adult who mimics looking okay with others, and the other is a crazy child who is not in reality. In order to heal and come into reality I had to go back to the womb (emotionally) and to birth (when I put my heart out of my body and under the floor to physically survive). Finally, after years of hard work, my *real* child began to grow and be in touch with reality. I'm conscious of my emotional insides more often, which means that I exist in reality more and more.

---

1 Dreamlike state between the conscious and the unconscious.
2 Repository of all unresolved issues and emotions of which we are not at all aware.

I continuously remind myself of the good people around me who love *all* of me, no matter how young I need to be to stay integrated. I've been doing this for a while, and recently a miracle happened. I no longer feel split vertically. Now I feel divided horizontally: conscious – subconscious – unconscious. I never had that before, and now for the first time I am experiencing it in reality. Something can be working in my subconscious and unconscious and then it shows up in my awareness the next day – and I was totally unaware of it until that moment. It feels like a miracle when that happens.

The definitions that make the most sense to me are the following: The unconscious is the deep repository of all unresolved feelings and experiences. The subconscious is the in-between state, the mediator between the conscious and the unconscious. Evidently, when something comes up to the subconscious it may manifest in a dream, or in thoughts. And so there is an element of the conscious in it, but it's drawing from the unconscious. Until you can pull things up from the unconscious with a process, you will not have access to it.

I had an exciting new experience yesterday. I had a nightmare. This was new, and it is a good sign because dreams are the language of the unconscious. So this is evidence that I am developing an unconscious. Now the unconscious and the subconscious are starting to do what they're supposed to, which is to work for me without any awareness of the process on my part. It is like an incredible miracle to me! I'm learning more about emotional tools for dealing with reality, which I have *never* experienced before. That is just the way I feel. I have begun to realize that when I am in reality, I feel I am bathed in white light; and even if it is unpleasant feelings, it feels like an unbelievable and miraculous experience to be in reality and to be able to feel.

Since I started developing a subconscious and an unconscious, I have kept myself open and ready to grow. And now sometimes a solution to a problem I was working on will pop up into my consciousness. I have never experienced that before! What an incredible gift!! Each time I find a new emotional tool for a problem, it makes my growth miraculously easier. I experience this as an original thought, even though I may have heard it many times before. My mom and I have some interesting conversations about this.

To a lesser degree, we all live in our own reality. Have you ever tried to get a child, friend, or student to see or learn something and they would not? Anyone who is working with someone coming out of schizophrenia must be aware that when he or she tells you that they are experiencing something for the first time, it is the truth; and as their guide, you must honor that.

Goodbyes

Now that I am in reality I am experiencing some losses. Kathleen and I would talk on the phone a lot, and we would talk about more adult things as I grew. She was a therapist so she could still deal with anything that showed up. Recently, I was at a place where I did not need her as much. I still enjoyed her, but I didn't need her. But then Kathleen died earlier last year (2024), and it's a *huge* loss. She accepted me wherever I was – a tiny baby needing to be held and given a bottle, needing a story read to me, or whatever. I had a hard time. I was afraid that a lot of my real self was dying with losing Kathleen. So I'm trying to figure that one out. I really worked hard for so many years to get into reality. And now in reality, I am experiencing some trauma. But it's okay that she's not physically here because I got a lot of what I needed from her.

And now I am having another new experience that is a bit shocking. My mom and dad got a divorce after 50 years of marriage. I was upset. I knew each of them were having a really hard time with this divorce, and because I've begun to individuate, I can experience what they are experiencing – and then separately what I'm experiencing. I'm working hard to give them all the space they need to deal with whatever they need to, and to be there for them as much as I can.

Then I was thinking about what it is that I need. I was kind of hurt about what I was not getting from my mom and dad, and that was new for me. And then I found myself pulling away. I've never experienced that before. Then I realized that if I do that all I'm doing is hurting myself because I'm putting up a wall between us. So I threw that response (pulling away) out the window. That was also a new experience.

Learning to Be

Bible verses were never real to me because words were not real to me. When I read a Bible verse I did not feel anything; they were just detached words. Since Dr. Hess was a minister, I knew all sorts of sayings from the Bible, but they were never real. As I have shared, a large part of my process of coming into reality is to continue to slow down. And as I have done that, some of the Bible verses that I know are now real to me. My favorite one is, "Be still and know that I am God."

It has been a long process of undoing many of the beliefs and programming that came from my childhood in the Hess family. I was taught that to enter heaven I had to believe in God and Jesus. But they were not real to me, so I thought that I would be sent to hell. Now that I have experienced healthy parents, I realize that God is a perfect parent and now I can believe in, and experience, God. I had always thought I had to put

God and Jesus in me in order to be a good Christian and go to heaven. It was like I would replace me with them to make me good. But as I have grown and moved away from the beliefs of my childhood, I can see that God and Jesus come into the real me (a good, warm, and healthy person) and we work together. I know now that I am not a horrible thing that needs to be replaced in order to get into heaven.

I recently heard someone say that I am light in human form. I can identify with that; it makes sense to me. I am part of the process – and I am good.

Mission Accomplished
by Christine E.

This mission of Shirana's might be called "Mission Impossible" by some, but I see Shirana's stepping into reality as nothing short of an unfolding miracle. Her growth in so many areas is exponentially rapid, while in other areas it is a steady progression toward a healthy ability to cope with life on life's terms.

A good example of this steady progression is Shirana's response to what recently happened with Christopher's death. He had a mobility crisis during this past month and got to a point where we called 911 and had him hospitalized. The bad news was that he was unable to stand, much less walk. The good news was that it may have been the result of being over-medicated, causing a steady decline of his muscle tone over the past year.

He was recently discharged from the hospital to a rehabilitation facility. His dosage on this medication was cut by 75 percent, which helped his mental acuity and his muscle tone, but he was in pretty bad shape. Christopher then unexpectedly died.

Through it all, Shirana has not split or taken any steps into psychosis. She has remained solidly in reality, and she was a steadfast advocate for Christopher in the rehab facility. She was a shining ray of light to both the staff and to Christopher. There are still big holes in her knowledge base in reality, but if you had asked me a year ago how she would have handled this crisis, it would not be like this! With continuing support, I am confident that she will not only make it through this crisis, but also grow even closer to personifying the angel of service that she is at the core of her being.

This Mission Impossible has become a path of Limitless potential and in many ways a mission accomplished – and hope for all those suffering from schizophrenia. Stay tuned for Part 2!!

Appendix A

What Is
Schizophrenia?

According to DSM-5 (*Diagnostic and Statistical Manual* (Fifth Edition), the characteristic symptoms of schizophrenia involve a range of cognitive, behavioral, and emotional dysfunctions, but no single symptom is pathognomonic of the disorder. The diagnosis involves the recognition of a constellation of signs and symptoms associated with impaired occupational or social functioning. Individuals with the disorder will vary substantially on most features, as schizophrenia is a heterogeneous clinical syndrome. Two (or more) of these symptoms must be present. At least one of these must be (1), (2), or (3):

1. Delusions
2. Hallucinations

3. Disorganized speech

4. Grossly disorganized or catatonic behavior

5. Negative symptoms (i.e., diminished emotional expression or avolition)

About the Author

Shirana Joy knew from the start that she had an assignment – an assignment from God. Although she did not know what the assignment was at the time, she now knows that it is to share with other schizophrenics how to come out of that black world of nothingness and into reality. *Growing the Real Me* is the realization of this assignment.

Christine E. currently works as a spiritual life coach after 30 years of counseling in private practice. She is a mother, grandmother, and great-grandmother, as well as the author of *Ascend to Joy*. Chris loves life, family, and helping others find their life purpose.